SPEEDBOATS
AT SEA

RICHARD AND LOUISE SPILSBURY

PowerKiDS
press.

New York

Published in 2018 by **The Rosen Publishing Group, Inc.**
29 East 21st Street, New York, NY 10010

Cataloging-in-Publication Data
Names: Spilsbury, Richard. | Spilsbury, Louise.
Title: Speedboats at sea / Richard and Louise Spilsbury.
Description: New York : PowerKids Press, 2018. | Series: Machines at sea | Includes index.
Identifiers: ISBN 9781499434538 (pbk.) | ISBN 9781499434484 (library bound) |
    ISBN 9781499434385 (6 pack)
Subjects: LCSH: Motorboats--Juvenile literature.
Classification: LCC GV835.S65 2018 | DDC 387.2'31--dc23

Produced for Rosen by Calcium
Editors for Calcium: Sarah Eason and Jennifer Sanderson
Designers for Calcium: Paul Myerscough and Jennie Child
Picture researcher: Harriet McGregor

Photo Credits: Cover: chang/E+/Getty Images. Inside: Seabreacher/Hydro Attack 29;
Shutterstock: Philip Bird LRPS CPAGB 4, Darren Brode 12, 13, ChameleonsEye 10,
EvrenKalinbacak 20, Angelo Giampiccolo 9, 31, Maxene Huiyu 28, Italianvideophotoagency 7,
18, Marcel Jancovic 15, Muratart 11, Nata-Lia 6, Normalfx 19, Ted PAGEL 27, Pres Panayotov
17, Portumen 16, Jan S. 5, Scanrail1 25, Barry Tuck 23, Ververidis Vasilis 22, Ints Vikmanis 26,
Chuck Wagner 21.

Manufactured in China
CPSIA Compliance Information: Batch BS17PK:
For Further Information contact Rosen Publishing, New York, New York at 1-800-237-9932.

SPEEDBOATS AT SEA

BOATS THAT SPEED!

Speedboats are unlike any other boats on the oceans. They are not designed to skim quietly and gracefully across the water's surface like sailing yachts. They do not carry many passengers comfortably like **ferryboats**, either. These boats are designed for one purpose only: to move at high speed.

The Need for Speed

Speedboats are small boats that are **powered** by engines. They are designed to go extremely fast and to be agile, or quick to turn and change direction, on the water. Speedboats were originally designed for pulling water skiers, to compete in races, to beat world speed records, and for other water competitions. When people saw how quick these boats were, they were soon used for other purposes, such as for patrolling coastlines and as military attack vehicles.

Speedboats are commonly used for water sports, including water-skiing and wakeboarding.

Speedboat Safety

Speedboats move quickly and can sometimes tip over, so safety is very important. Everyone on a speedboat should wear a life jacket. This is a device inflated with gas, so that it floats and keeps the wearer's head above water should he or she fall in. The wearer can breathe if he or she is unconscious.

KILL SWITCH

In an open vessel, the speedboat driver should wear a kill switch cord. This is a piece of curly plastic wire that clips onto the driver's leg and attaches to an on/off switch on the boat. If the driver is thrown from the boat, the cord pulls out of the switch, and the engine stops working. The boat then slows down quickly, and there is less danger of the boat's engine harming the person in the water.

Racers in speedboats often wear helmets and life jackets for protection against impacts if they are thrown into the water.

HOW SPEEDBOATS WORK

Speedboats can plow across the ocean at high speeds only because of hidden **forces**. Forces are pushes and pulls that make things move. They work in pairs, so for every force in one direction, there is another in the opposite direction.

Balanced Forces

A speedboat can float because of a balanced pair of forces. The **weight** of a boat is caused by the pull of gravity on its mass. Gravity is the pull of every object downward toward the center of Earth. A force called **upthrust** balances this force. Upthrust is the upward push on the boat from seawater on the boat's shape. If upthrust and weight are not balanced, then the speedboat will sink.

Boats float on water because of forces acting on them that result from the vessel's weight and the ocean's water.

How fast a speedboat goes depends on differences between thrust and drag forces.

Unbalanced Forces

The boat moves forward because of an unbalanced pair of forces. One is called **thrust**. For an average speedboat, this is the push of a **propeller** powered by its engine. The spinning propeller pushes backward on the water behind the boat. This makes the boat move forward in the water. The faster the propeller spins, the greater the thrust, and the faster the boat moves. The force opposing thrust is water resistance, or **drag**. This is the backward force of the seawater pushing against the front, sides, and bottom of the boat as it moves forward. A speedboat travels fast because its thrust is greater than the drag.

SPEED AND ACCELERATION

Speed, or **velocity,** is how fast something is going, and acceleration is a change in the velocity. Acceleration usually means that something moves faster and faster. Without drag, a speedboat would keep accelerating.

SHAPED FOR SPEED

One of the first things we notice about a speedboat is that it has a pointed front and smooth, curved sides. This **streamlined** shape helps it move quickly.

What a Drag

Speedboats have to work against different types of drag. **Skin** friction is a type of drag caused by the interaction between water and the skin of the boat. Form drag is caused by the push of water against the boat's front shape. A larger area means more form drag. Wave drag is caused by the battling water directions in waves pushed out of the way at the front and sides of the boat. A sharp point, or **bow**, at the front cuts through the water well, reducing form and wave drag. The smooth sides and long, thin shape of a speedboat reduce skin friction.

What Lies Beneath?

The design of a boat's **hull** also affects how it works. A curved shape behind the bow acts a little like an airplane wing. Moving forward causes an upward push. This then reduces form drag. To reduce drag, some speedboats have flat bottoms that get on top of the water easily. However, they can lack control because there are fewer sideways forces to hold the line. Many speedboats have sharp **keels**, so that they keep direction better at speed.

DRAG, SPEED, AND AREA

Drag increases with speed. That is because the faster the object moves, the greater the opposite force. Drag also increases with area. When you dive into a pool, you point your arms forward to make a streamlined shape. This reduces the area contacting the water. If you do a belly flop and hit the water flat, it hurts.

Waves at the sides of the speedboat are a sign of drag. The sharp bow has little drag because of its shape.

9

JET BOATS

Jet boats are speedboats with a difference. These boats do not use the thrust from a spinning propeller. Instead, jet boats use the force of a jet of water to speed along.

Boating Is a Blast

On the bottom of a jet boat's hull, water is sucked in using a **pump** powered by the engine. Spinning parts in the engine increase the **water pressure**. This pressure is the force that pushes water through the engine's pipes. The high-pressure water blasts out of one or several nozzles at the back, or **stern**, of the boat, just at water level. It is the powerful water jet pushing out against the water behind the boat that makes it move forward.

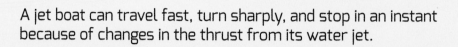

A jet boat can travel fast, turn sharply, and stop in an instant because of changes in the thrust from its water jet.

Maneuvering

Conventional speedboats have a fixed propeller position. They change direction using a vertical fin, called a rudder, behind the propeller. Angling the rudder one way means that the thrust from the propeller against it pushes the boat the other way. On jet boats, changing the direction that the water jet points in steers the boat.

A propeller can spin in the opposite way to put a normal speedboat into reverse. On a jet boat, a deflector plate is lowered behind the water jet. The plate deflects the water jet down and forward, rather than backward, so the jet boat reverses or keeps stationary in the water.

JET SKIS

Jet skis are like the fast, agile motorcycles of the sea. They are powered just like jet boats. The main difference is that people sit on top of Jet skis and steer them with handlebars, rather than sitting inside and using a steering wheel.

Jet skis are shorter, more maneuverable jet boats for one or two people.

HYDROPLANES

Hydroplanes are a type of boat that are a little like jet airplanes. They use the push of air and water from below to lift them as high as possible out of the water. This reduces drag, so they can reach incredible speeds.

Shaped to Rise

Most hydroplanes have two narrow hulls, called sponsons, at the sides, with a gap under the boat. The sponsons channel air under the boat as it moves forward. The air forced in at high speed pushes the sponsons up, so that they almost rise completely from the water. The front of the boat is flying!

You can see a space under a hydroplane at speed because it is mostly above the water to reduce drag.

LEFT TURN ONLY

Hydroplanes have a large metal blade, called a skid fin, sticking vertically into the water from the left sponson. At speed, hydroplanes turn without toppling over by using the skid fin as a pivot in the water. There is no fin on the right-hand side, so these boats cannot turn right.

At low speed, hydroplanes are not great because there is no air or water lift. The heavy engine then makes the hull sink into the water.

Extra Lift

Remember how water hitting the curved shape of a normal speedboat's hull can push it upward? Hydroplanes take this effect to its extremes. The central part of the hull, containing the massive engine and the pilot, has a wide piece, called a ram wing, underneath. The angle of the ram wing helps make the hull lift, too. The driver can operate a foot pedal to change the angle to lift the boat more or less, depending on how choppy the water is.

Rooster Tail

The only part of the stern of a speeding hydroplane that is always in the water is its propeller. At high speeds, the boat lifts so much that the propeller is partly sticking above the surface. The fast-spinning propeller can throw a curved spurt of white water up to hundreds of feet long. This is called the rooster tail.

BOATS USING AIR

Some speedboats have flat bottoms. They move across water or onto land. These boats do not have propellers or water jets for thrust. Instead, they use air to move along.

Airboats

In marshy places with shallow waterways, such as the Everglades in Florida, it is not unusual to hear the sound of a large fan approaching. This is the fan of an airboat. An airboat is a flat boat with an airplane propeller mounted on the back, pointing backward. This provides the forward thrust. This type of speedboat is ideal in places where water plants could snag around propellers or where water is so shallow that the bottom of a normal boat would hit the ground. On an airboat, there is nothing sticking into the water. Even the rudder is fitted behind the fan.

Hovercraft

Air-cushion vehicles (ACVs), or **hovercraft**, float along on water or land on their own bubble of air. These vehicles have downward-pointing fans on board. The fans blow down high-pressure air into the space underneath the hovercraft. Here, flexible rubber walls around the craft form a deep skirt, which is inflated by the air. Air can get out under the edges of the skirt, but the pressure underneath the hovercraft is greater than that in the air around it, so the boat lifts upward.

HAIRDRYER MOMENT

In the early twentieth century, Christopher Cockrell invented the hovercraft. He devised an air cushion to lift a boat after experimenting with a hairdryer to blow air into one tin can inside a slightly larger one.

A hovercraft floats on an air cushion but moves forward like an airboat by using large onboard fans or propellers for thrust.

SPEEDBOAT MATERIALS

The first speedboats were made of wood, which is a strong material that floats well. Wood can be shaped and bent into streamlined boat shapes. However, wood is heavy and gradually rots in seawater. Today, speedboats are mostly made from other man-made materials.

Plastics

Many speedboats are made from strong, lightweight, waterproof, rotproof plastics. The plastic used for many boats is known as **fiberglass** because it is usually reinforced with tiny fibers of glass that mesh the plastic together. The toughest plastics for their weight that are used for speedboats are Kevlar and carbon fiber.

BOAT BUILDING

Fiberglass hulls are quicker to make than wooden ones. The basic process is laying fiberglass cloth in a boat-shaped mold and then soaking it in liquid plastic. Once it is set hard, with a bit of sanding and adjusting, the boat is ready.

The curved, drag-resistant hulls of most speedboats are made from plastics.

Metals

Speedboats that operate under the most powerful ocean forces could shatter if they were made from plastics. That is why these speedboats have hulls made from aluminum alloys. Alloys are mixes of metals that combine their properties. Aluminum is a light metal but not very strong. Mixing in other metals, such as magnesium, make it much stronger. Many parts of speedboats are made from alloys, too. These include rustproof, strong stainless steel, which is used for rails, and cast metals, such as brass, for tough propellers.

RIBs are light, powerful, and stable enough to carry many passengers.

RIBs

RIB stands for "rigid inflatable boat." These boats have a solid, plastic hull with a ring of inflatable tubes around the edge of the top. Air-filled tubes are very light compared to solid materials. They are also very **buoyant**. RIB speedboats can cope with rough seas because they float so well, even if a wave breaks over them.

ENGINE POWER

Most speedboats use engines to spin propellers in the water. Boaters usually make the engine go faster or slower using a lever, called a throttle, by the steering wheel.

In or Out

Some speedboat engines are **inboard**. This means that the body of the engine is built into the inside of the boat, with the propeller shaft sticking out of the bottom toward the stern. Other boat engines are **outboard**. Here the engine and the propeller form a separate unit attached to the stern. Inboard engines are quieter than outboard engines. However, they are fixed in place, so they are difficult to change to increase the power. Outboard engines can be changed easily. However, because the fast-spinning propeller is at the back on an outboard engine, it can be a hazard for water skiers and other people doing water sports.

Inboard engines mean there is space at the stern to sit and to easily climb in and out when the boat stops.

The Power

Engines on speedboats have different amounts of power to make them go fast. Bigger, heavier boats need more power to make them go faster than smaller, lighter boats. Big engines are heavy, so they could weigh down a very light boat. An engine's power is measured in **horsepower** (hp). Engines for smaller speedboats are upward of 15 hp, but the biggest can be up to 1,000 hp. Some superfast boats may have several engines to reach maximum power.

KEEPING IN TRIM

"Trim" is the word used to mean the angle of an outboard engine and its propeller in the water. "Trimmed in" means the propeller is pointing downward in the water, and "trimmed out" means it is pointing upward. Speedboat users can change the trim, for example, when the boat is loaded up or when the sea has high waves to keep the propeller in the water, so that it produces maximum power.

If each of these engines were 200 hp, the total engine power of this boat would be 600 hp.

SPEEDBOATS FOR RACING

People who like to race speedboats say there is nothing like the rush of **adrenaline** you get from zooming across the water at high speed, trying to beat your competitors. There are speedboat races all over the world, and there are many different kinds of race.

Different Races

Speedboat races can be fast and furious, but endurance races can last up to an hour and cover more than 100 miles (161 km) or in some cases even 500 miles (805 km). There are different races for boats with inboard or outboard engines. People race across lakes and offshore along coasts. In many races, there is only one driver per boat. In offshore racing, the boats can be more than 50 feet (15 m) long and are usually run by a driver and another crewmember to control the power to the engine.

Offshore powerboat races are usually point-to-point, from one place to another, and spectators watch from the shore or from stationary boats.

HIGH-SPEED RACING

Some hydroplane speedboats are powered by a massive Chinook helicopter engine and can race along at more than 200 miles per hour (321 km/h) on straight stretches of a race.

The Formula 1 Powerboat World Championship is an international motorboat racing competition that is similar to Formula 1 car racing.

Safety at Speed

Finding the right balance between speed and safety is vital for speedboat racers. Race drivers should keep a good lookout for other boats and take action to avoid collisions. They also need to keep an eye on the waves and wash from other boats, which could cause them to tilt or tip over. They should also avoid going too hard into corners and when changing direction, since this can lead to them **capsizing**. In speedboat racing, the driver of the boat may sit inside a **cockpit**, which is reinforced so that if the boat does capsize, it does not get crushed, and the driver will be safe.

SPEEDBOATS FOR FUN

Many speedboats are designed solely to go fast, with space only for a minimal crew. That may be fine for racing, but some people want to use speedboats for fun and even be able to stay on them for long periods of time.

Fast and Fun

Some speedboats may have a cabin with a large space for a bed, so that people can speed across the water and stay overnight on their vessel. Other boats may have no cabin but are big enough to have 12 or more passenger seats. This means that boat owners can take their friends and family out on the boat. Many speedboats are used to tow inflatables. These range from giant rubber tubes to those shaped like bananas. People sit on these and are pulled over the waves as the speedboat in front tows them along.

Riders must grip tightly to handles on inflatable floats, as they bounce over the water pulled behind a speedboat.

Time to Wake Up!

Speedboats have different designs, depending on what sport they are used for. A wakeboarding boat needs to create a large wake behind it. A **wake** is the trail of disturbed water or waves that a boat kicks up when it passes through. A good wakeboarding boat has to shift a lot of water out of the way as it travels. One way it does this is with extra **ballast** weight to make the boat heavy. The engine is usually placed backward in the rear of the boat, in order to keep more weight in the back and to increase the size of the wake.

WIELDING A WEDGE

A wedge is a flat wing on a pole. This device extends just below the water at the stern of the boat to increase form drag and, therefore, the size of the wake.

The very large trails and waves created by wakeboard boats help wakeboarders launch high into the air, as they jump side to side behind the boat.

SPEEDBOATS FOR RESCUE

Sea rescues are needed when sailors fall overboard, when fishermen are injured on the water, or when boats capsize or are damaged. Rescue speedboats, or lifeboats, have several technological innovations that help them do their job.

Trouble at Sea

Speedboats used to rescue people have to be fast and tough. Most accidents and problems on the water happen in bad weather, so these vessels must be able to cope with the most demanding conditions. The boats often have an aluminum alloy hull. This is lightweight to make them go fast but also tough enough to withstand impacts from powerful and high-breaking waves.

The Bridge

Many rescue boats have an enclosed bridge, or survivor compartment, on top of the boat. This has heavy-duty, watertight doors and windows that resist damage and stop flooding, so that the rescue team inside is safe if the boat tips over. The engines are also special heavy-duty machines that can cope with being turned over completely and fully submerged in water.

BUOYANCY CHAMBERS

In rough seas, there is a real risk that boats will be tipped over by the waves. Many rescue boats have buoyancy chambers that give the vessel a self-righting capability. This means that they will immediately roll back to an upright position after being turned over.

Some lifeboats are painted in bright colors, so that they can be seen and identified easily by other rescue vehicles in bad weather and high waves.

SPEEDBOATS ON PATROL

Speedboats are also used to patrol the waters around coastlines and shores to catch criminals operating at sea.

Harbor Patrol

Although speedboats are mainly used for racing and for fun, they are sometimes used by criminals to do things that are against the law. For example, people use them to **smuggle** illegal substances, such as narcotics, quickly across international waters. Criminals also used speedboats to outrun the Coast Guard or other authorities. Today, however, coast guard crews and law enforcement agencies use superfast boats and helicopters to keep up with and catch such criminals.

MULTIPLE JOBS

Speedboats on patrol do a variety of jobs. They check ships arriving at ports, catch boats that are carrying people trying to enter a country illegally, catch smugglers, and perform search-and-rescue jobs. They also respond when there are accidents, such as **oil spills,** in the water.

A large harbor speedboat on drill in Singapore practices approaching a smaller boat to arrest the occupants and seize their cargo.

This US Coast Guard armed defender class boat is 25 feet (8 m) long. It is a tough, armored RIB.

Built for Action

Boats carrying people who may have to face dangerous criminals must be equipped for action. Many can go from zero to high speed in fewer than 4 seconds and travel at more than 40 **knots**. They are usually fairly small, so they are lighter and can go faster in order to respond faster to callouts. To improve their speed, many also have several high-powered outboard engines. Most are RIBs with inflatable collars that keep a boat level, steady, and safe, even during high-speed chases or when a big wave floods them. These boats are also designed to help the navy in times of war, so they are equipped with weapons. Some have guns mounted both forward and backward on the boat.

SPEEDBOATS OF THE FUTURE

In the future, speedboats will stay in demand because people like or need to travel fast across water. However, new technology is changing what these boats will be like and how they will work.

Robot Boats

Military personnel driving fast speedboats into conflict situations can be in great danger. That is why the first robot speedboats have already been built. These have no drivers or passengers. People using remote controls operate them from a safe distance away.

Armed robot RIB speedboats like this could become a regular part of naval operations in the future.

FlyShips

FlyShips are part speedboat, part airplane, and part hovercraft. They use huge fans and wide wings to create a cushion over the waves. At present they are not widely used, but they could become a common sight on the oceans in the future.

DIFFERENT POWER

In the future, speedboats may get their power from the sun, rather than from gas-guzzling engines. They will have **solar cells** on top that convert the sun's energy into electricity to spin their propellers.

Bubble Boats

Speedboats in the future could ride on bubbles to go faster using less effort. Layers of bubbles under a boat can act like grease, helping it move faster past the surrounding water. Air-supported vessels could use their bow shape to make streams of bubbles to go faster. New engines may also have special systems to stream bubbles around propellers, so that they can spin faster than they are able to with the drag of still water.

Underwater Speedboat!

The Seabreacher is an incredibly fast, streamlined jet boat that can dive underwater and shoot up into the air something like a dolphin. The pilot inside the cockpit uses levers to make the boat roll, leap, and spin, which gives the passenger the ride of his life!

A Seabreacher is a short, highly maneuverable jet boat built for fun!

GLOSSARY

adrenaline A substance that is released in a person's body that makes their heart beat faster and gives them more energy.

ballast A weight, such as water, added to a boat to make it more stable.

bow The front of the boat's hull.

buoyant Able to float.

capsizing Turning over in the water.

cockpit The protected space with instruments inside, where the pilot of a vehicle sits to operate it.

drag The force of friction between a moving object and the substance, such as water, through which it moves.

ferryboats Boats that are used to carry people and things for a short distance between two places.

fiberglass A material made from plastic that is reinforced with tiny glass fibers.

forces Pushes or pulls that can change the way things move.

horsepower The unit of measurement of engine power.

hovercraft A machine that reduces drag with water or land by floating and moving along on a cushion of air above it.

hull The bottom of a boat.

inboard Describes a motor built into a boat.

keels Structures along the centerline at the bottom of vessels' hulls, on which the rest of the hull is built. In some boats, the keel extends as a blade to make the boats stable.

knots Nautical miles per hour: 1 nautical mile is equivalent to about 1.2 miles per hour (2 km/h).

oil spills When oil spills onto water or land, often causing a mess, pollution, and harm to living things.

outboard Describes a motor attached to the outside of a boat.

power The rate of doing work; a tractor has more power than a lawnmower.

propeller A machine with angled blades that spins to create thrust in water or air.

pump A device to suck in liquid.

skin A sheathing or casing forming the outside surface of a boat.

smuggle To transport goods illegally, often hidden.

solar cells Devices that convert energy in sunlight into electrical energy.

stern The back of a boat, which is often blunt, not pointed.

streamlined Describes something that is shaped to reduce drag when moving through water or air.

thrust A pushing force in one direction.

upthrust The force pushing objects up in liquid. It is also known as buoyancy.

velocity The distance moved in a period of time. It is also known as speed.

wake Streams of waves behind a moving boat caused by its drag on water.

water pressure The push of water on the surface of any object.

weight The effect of gravity on the mass of an object.

FURTHER READING

Books

Hauenstein, Michael. *Speedboat Racers.* Enslow Publishers, 2010.

Tougias, *Michael J. A Storm Too Soon: A Remarkable True Survival Story in 80 Foot Seas.* Square Fish, 2017.

Von Finn, Denny. *Powerboats* (Torque: World's Fastest). Bellwether, 2016.

Websites

Due to the changing nature of Internet links, PowerKids Press has developed an online list of websites related to the subject of this book. This site is updated regularly. Please use this link to access the list: www.powerkidslinks.com/mas/speedboats

INDEX